THE TIME BENDER

Keys to Unlocking and Restoring Time

DANIEL PRINGLE SR

THE TIME BENDER

Keys to Unlocking and Restoring Time

By Daniel Pringle Sr.

To contact the author:
Daniel Pringle Ministries
P.O. Box 195313
Dallas, TX 75219
www.danielpringle.com

Cover design
Tanner Gary
www.absolutgraphics.org

All rights reserved solely by the author. No part of this book may be reproduced, stored in a retrieval system or transmitted by any means without the written permission of the author. Unless otherwise states, all quotations are taken the King James Version of the Bible.

Copyright © 2014 by Daniel Pringle
All rights reserved.
ISBN-13: 978-1495977657

DANIEL PRINGLE SR

DEDICATION

I want to thank my wife, Tammy, and my sons, Daniel Jr., and Phillip, for their encouragement. With all the setbacks I have experienced in life, you have continued to support me.

CONTENTS

	Introduction...	1
1	Buy Back Season..	3
2	Misplaced Time...	12
3	Seasons of Restoration...	19
4	The Harvest Factor	32
5	Unexpected Harvest...	37
6	A Healthy Soul	47
7	Moving Into Overflow...	67

INTRODUCTION

Has anyone really lived their life exactly the way that he or she planned? Probably not, but it does not mean your days are wasted. Our lives are a journey full of detours, delays and even, unexpected disruptions. Regardless of life's speed bumps, God has a plan for everyone, including you. He also has a season that has been earmarked to fulfill that plan. In every season, there are opportunities with doors designed to move you through to obtain the harvest God has for your life. One of the secrets in life is learning to navigate through those doors and how to move to the next season being fruitful in every area.

However, what do you do when bad decisions cause you to miss opportunities or events beyond your control? Do you feel that your life is behind schedule? When you feel behind schedule, there always comes a sense of urgency to catch up. You see other people progressing but you believe you are not where you should be. In Psalm 31:15, King David said *"My times are in your hands."* Time is a servant that has been created for your purpose to be realized. In the book of Joel, God says that He will *restore to you the years the locusts have eaten*. In other words, it is possible to redeem time lost and recover missed opportunities.

In two specific occurrences, the Word of God shows where time was (literally) altered. In Joshua 10, we find Joshua in a battle with the Amorites. He was in a situation where he needed more time to accomplish what God had called him to do. The only negative thing that could have prevented him was that the sun was starting to go down. If the sun had set, then the Amorites would have been able to retreat and recover. Joshua was able to recognize this historic moment and did something no man had done previously. He commanded the sun to stand still. Through Joshua's faith and his bold declaration, time was momentary suspended.

Second, in the story of King Hezekiah—the prophet told him that he was going to die soon. After delivering him this message and leaving the king's presence, God spoke to a prophet and told him that He was going to add another 15 years to King Hezekiah's life. As a sign that God was going to add years to the king, the shadow (or the clock's dial) moved back 15 degrees. God moved, or can I say, God *bent time*. By bending time, God gave King Hezekiah 15 more years.

This is what I call, a "buy back season," where we can redeem lost time, and once you learn the principals of *time*, God will release an unexpected harvest, and create a custom tailored season designed just for you. If you have lost years through unfortunate circumstances and feel that it is too late—it is not. God is a God of restoration and redemption. This book can prepare you and teach you the keys to unlocking and restoring time, so that you recover missed opportunities in order for you to experience the harvest prepared just for you.

1

Buy Back Season

THE 1990s WAS A BOOMING time in the US with the explosion of the internet industry and a flourishing economy. Many people became very wealthy during the "dot com" era, even at a young age. Young people coming out of college were able to secure great paying jobs. At the same time, the real estate market was thriving with extremely low interest rates. For many, who saw renting as their only option, were suddenly able to buy a home. If you owned a home, it was prime time for a second mortgage to do remodeling, additions, or to upgrade to a larger home. With new regulations and conditions for qualifications, private mortgage companies began lending money to people that did not have good credit. Eventually, the bubble burst.

People, who thought they were living the American dream, found out that they were in over their heads with mortgages, credit cards, and car loans that they could no longer afford. The private mortgage companies that were lending money with very loose criteria were now financially unstable. What once was a secure economy, suddenly the market crashed. Greed took over and CEO's of major companies exposed of illegal and immoral practices were facing legal ramifications. Overnight, companies went out of business. The nation was faced with high volumes of job losses and bank foreclosures. To prevent a national crisis, government bailouts for major corporations materialized, which resulted in a widespread global economic meltdown.

Individuals that were on the brink of retiring lost their pensions and people had to change careers or go back to school in order to get a new job. Some took pay cuts just to keep their jobs. Countless people who lost their homes to foreclosure and bankruptcy began to abandon cities, as factories and companies closing in hope for finding a fresh start. The Bible says, *"Hope deferred makes the heart heavy, but when the dream comes it is the tree of life."* (Prov.13:12).

All of the financial distress that plagued our nation has affected lives either directly or indirectly. Many people that spent years on a job, invested their life in the company found themselves unemployed. The real estate market crashed. Lending companies gave borrowers homes for more than what they could afford, which caused many people to lose their homes. It is more difficult now than ever to purchase a home because of the new lending requirements imposed by banking institutions. We have looked to the government to change policies so that the American people can get their dreams back. As a result, many people Band-Aid stimulus incentives to jump-start the economy.

Maybe some type of loss has affected you or someone you know in your life whether financially, through a job layoff, a company shutdown, a loss of a home, or you may have ended up in a bad relationship. Let me tell you something, in the midst of your meltdown, God still has a plan for you.

> *"For I know the thoughts that I think toward you, says the Lord, thoughts of peace and not of evil, to give you a future and a hope.* (Jer. 29: 11).

God's plans are not affected by the economy, nor is it affected by life interruptions. Just because the economy in our nation has changed does not mean that God has changed His plans, nor does it mean that He needs to come up with an alternate strategy.

God has a destiny for your life that includes an awesome future. No matter what you are going through at the present, you still have a future. A future filled with peace and hope. A future that is glorious. You cannot do anything about what you have experienced in the past, but God is creating a brand new future for you. God has a plan of recovery for your life and He has not stopped thinking about you for one second.

God is thinking about you and your future so much that David said they are more than can be numbered.

"Many, O Lord my God, are thy wonderful works which thou hast done, And thy thoughts which are to us-ward: they cannot be reckoned up in order unto thee: If I would declare and speak of them, they are more than can be numbered." (Ps. 40:5).

I often say, "If you could just get one thought from God, your whole life would change." All you need is one thought. Yet, the thoughts of God towards you are so numerous that it is impossible to count them all. When you think it is over, He is still thinking about you. While you are asleep, He is still thinking about you. When you feel like giving up, He is still thinking about you.

Let me say this to you, no matter what type of a loss you have experienced in life, God is able to restore to you the years that have been lost.

"Be glad then, ye children of Zion, and rejoice in the Lord your God: For he hath given you the former rain moderately, And he will cause to come down for you the rain, The former rain, and the latter rain in the first month. And the floors shall be full of wheat, and the fats shall overflow with wine and oil. And I will restore to you the years that the locust hath eaten, the cankerworm, and the caterpillar, and the palmerworm, My great army which I sent among you. And ye shall eat in plenty, and be satisfied, and praise the name of the Lord your God that hath dealt wondrously with you: And my people shall never be ashamed. And ye shall know that I am in the midst of Israel, And that I am the Lord your God, and none else: And my people shall never be ashamed." (Joel 2:23-27).

It is not too late for you to recover. It does not matter how many years you lost, He is able to restore every year back to you. God is in the business of restoration and He is good at it. Whether you realize it or not, right now God is in the process of restoring to you the years that you have lost. Paul says, *"See then that ye walk circumspectly, not as fools, but as wise, redeeming the time, because the days are evil."* (Eph. 5:15).

We are called to redeem time. In other words, we are to make the most of our opportunities. In order for you to get where you want to be in life, you are going to need a door of opportunity. Many people have not advanced in life because they did not make the most of the opportunities presented to them. Therefore, they were not able to retrieve "out of time" the opportunities available for them to advance. When God is ready to advance you, He will give you an opportunity. That opportunity comes in a season. You do not have to backslide completely to be ineffective and unproductive. All the enemy wants is for you to miss your season.

By moving too early and not being prepared, you can miss your season. You can also miss your season by being too late. As a result, you are always trying to play catch up.

It is important for you to recognize your season. By not recognizing the season you are in, you can miss your opportunity. When in a sowing season, you think that you should be in a reaping season. When you miss your season, you will not retrieve the fruit designated for that season. Even if you have missed your seasons in life, God wants to redeem time. Redeem means "to buy up, to rescue from loss and improve opportunity."

The losses in life are not gone. They can be rescued. If you want to have time *unlocked* so that you can have time *restored*, the place for you to start for new opportunities begins with a thorough understanding of the will of God for your life. *"Wherefore be ye not unwise, but understanding what the will of the Lord is,"* (Eph. 5:15). God's will in your life is designed to be expressed in times and seasons. David said, *"So teach us to number our days, that we may apply our hearts unto wisdom."* (Ps. 90:10-12).

Only when we understand the *value* of time can we *redeem* time. Therefore, we need to ask God to teach us to number our days. Understanding the gift of time will enable us to express the will of God in the earth. You have a certain amount of time in which to do what God has called you to do. You cannot afford to be unaware of seasons and opportunities.

I believe we are entering into a tremendous season of restoration. We are in a "buy back season" where a sovereign God is beginning to orchestrate things to such a degree where we can buy back time and opportunities. He is giving us a moment, a period of time that has been marked out by Him. God said that He would restore the years . . . not the days, weeks or months, but He would restore years that were lost. Have you lost years in your life that you wish you could recover?

I have personally seen God bend and restore time in my own life. By being out of position, doing the wrong thing and making poor choices, it has greatly affected my life negatively. Nevertheless, I have good news. It does not take God twelve years to make up for the last twelve years of mistakes in your life. He has a season called "suddenly" that begins to expedite time and give you back retroactive pay. A *suddenly season* is when something enters from eternity *into* time, without any prior announcement. Because God is not obligated by time, He is never in a hurry. What we call "suddenly" is not a suddenly to God. Everything God does, He premeditates with great consideration, thought, and planning. If one day is like 1000 years and 1000 years is like one day, then what we call a suddenly breakthrough has been in the process for 1000 years in the mind of God. So when a *suddenly season* arrives, you enter into the "action mode" of what God had been previously premeditated and planned.

Time is a very interesting concept. Defined, time is a component, a quantity of many measurements in a sequence of events. To compare the durations of events and the intervals between them is very complicated. Time is a measurement between a series of events. Without any measurements, there would be not use of time. Time is passing non-stop, and we follow it with clocks and calendars. Yet we cannot study it with a microscope or experiment with it. Yet, it still keeps passing. We cannot say what exactly happens when time passes.

In time, there are three stages, the past, the present, and the future. As time passes, the future becomes your present and your present becomes your past. Before God created the heavens and the earth, there was no time. There was only God and thus, we say that God is eternal. God is not in time, but rather time is in God. Time is universal. Every person has the same amount of time, twenty-four hours a day. Regardless of nationality, financial status, gender, or age, time does not discriminate. We all live in a timeframe with 365 days a year, twenty-four hours a day, sixty minutes each hour, and sixty seconds per minute. The only variable is how many of those years you get and the only person that knows how many years you get is God.

Have you ever wondered why God created time in the first place? I think that there are many reasons why God created time. One of those reasons is that it prevents everything from happening all at once. God takes pleasures in watching things develop, watching things grow, and watching things come to a place of maturity. In order for your purpose to be processed, God created time. Through time, each person has a unique purpose to process. Yes, there are times when God can accelerate the process and bring you into what I call a "suddenly season." However, God is not in a hurry, even though we are, because God never runs out of time.

The Bible says, *"Since his days are determined, the number of his months is with You; You have appointed his limits so that he cannot pass."* (Job 14:5). Because you have been given a certain amount of time, time now becomes valuable. Your time is valuable. Everything is competing for your time . . . your job, family, friends, traffic, etc. What we do not realize is the value of time as it relates even to our finances. Two extremely important elements that we possess are time and money. They are important because of their fundamental value.

There is a relationship between time and money. If someone employs you, they are paying you for your time. Your employer is telling you what one hour of your time is worth to their company. Therefore, if they may pay you $20 an hour, they set a value on your "hour" or 60 minutes of your life. They are giving your $20 for an hour of your time in order to perform a certain task or assignment for their company. You may feel as though your time is worth more than what you are being paid for, but it is the value of what your employer proposes. When you want more money for your time to perform the same task, you ask for an increase in pay.

The world we live places a value on time and money, and currency evaluates the assessment. It takes money to do things, live, eat, etc. Many people are not earning enough money to do what they desire and so they may opt to get a second job. I have found that one way to make more money is not necessarily in working two jobs, but rather by increasing your personal value. Your personal value can increase through acquiring new skill sets or by obtaining an education. *"If an ax is blunt and the edge isn't sharpened, then one has to use more strength. But wisdom prepares the way for success."* (Eccl. 10:10). Increasing your personal value makes you an asset that others will be willing to pay. You are paid for what you are worth rather than what your employer can afford to pay you.

The older you get, there is less risks you can afford to take. In other words, when you are younger, you take more financial risks because if something goes wrong you have more time to make it up. If you are older, you do not have the luxury to take as many financial risks as you did when you were younger. For instance, you may take a risk quitting one job and take another with the hopes that the new job will be promising. If that does not work out you still have plenty time to recoup your losses. This idea does not pertain to money only, but the older you are, you generally do not have the latitude to make bad decisions because you do not have the time to recover your losses. In upcoming chapters, we will see how this concept of time and finances is relevant to buying back time, but for now, I want to show the value of both time and money.

2

Misplaced Time

IF YOU DO NOT UNDERSTAND the value of time, you will end up wasting, mismanaging, or killing time. One of the most frustrating things is the feeling that you are behind time. We lose time, run out of time, and pass the time. Being behind time puts you in an awkward position where you feel, as though are you in a continual rat race to catch up. If a person has not taken an appraisal of their lives, he or she usually feels they are behind time. A life appraisal may include the following: where are you, what you have accomplished, how far you have come, and a mental comparison with others of similar age. When you take the time to look at your life and you discover that you should be much further than where you are right now, it can be very frustrating. To be behind time, behind the schedule of your life is overwhelming.

When your life is not where you thought it would be it places a demand to hurry up and do something. Interruptions in life can cause you to lose time and get behind. Maybe you had every intention of going to college after high school, but because the money was not there, and you had to pay your own way. No matter how hard you tried and worked at it, the money was just not there, so you dropped out of college never completing your education. Now you find yourself working on a job that does not interest you. You fell into something that has nothing to do with your desires. Now that you have been in it for so long, that you cannot afford to just quit and go back to school because you have bills to pay, you are married and you have started a family. What you are doing and the career you are in was not what you had planned when you were younger.

Life has progressed and you feel that you should be at a certain place . . . settled and comfortable in life. You have a car, furniture, a house and you are able to take vacations. Then, another life interruption shows up that knocks you backwards and sends you into a transition back where you were 10 years prior. It can be extremely exasperating. Imagine working on a job for years, and now you have to go back to school, starting all over to get the skills that you didn't get before. It is maddening. It is not just you anymore. Now you are married and have children to support. It is not as easy to go back to school now that you are forty years old, as when you were twenty. When you are in that place, there is an unvarying internal drive within your heart to catch up.

What makes people feel that they are behind time? What is the measurement you use to determine where you are supposed to be at a certain time in your life? So often, people look at others who appear to have it all together, especially when they are in the same age group. They appear to have a level of success that you are not experiencing. Too often, when people compare themselves with others, an alarm goes off, letting you know that you are not where you should be. Then you are faced with this realization, somehow, you missed it. You missed your opportunity and time is getting away. Many people have well thought out plans and goals with deadlines attached to them, but for some unexpected reason interruptions occurred that caused them to get off course, and now they feel defeated and unfilled.

Many factors in our lives have not only shaped you into who

you are, but have also cost you many priceless years. It would be nice if you could just reschedule your life and everything goes back to how you planned it. The older you get, the more you begin to see the value of time. One of the reasons that you are not where you "think" that you should be is because there have been circumstances; some beyond your control, some within your control, that had a great impact upon your life. Those circumstances cost you weeks, months and even years.

One bad decision can cost you years. This is why time is so very important. Once time is gone, you cannot go back and retrieve it. However, I do have some good news for you. Even though you cannot go back and retrieve time, you have a God that is a *time bender* and He is able to *restore* to you the years that have been lost.

In chapter one, I quoted from the book of Joel, *"And I will restore to you the years that the locust hath eaten,"* (2:24). Joel was a prophet to the southern kingdom of Judah (835-796 BC), about the same time Elisha was prophesying to the Northern Kingdom, in Israel (848 BC). Joel spoke to people who had become very complacent and self-centered. They took God for granted and worshiped idols. They had become insensitive to the condition of their spiritual lives, so Joel warned them that eventually their sinful lifestyles would bring down the judgment of God. Yet, they seemed oblivious to their spiritual need. Why did they need God? Up to this time, they had been experiencing a great abundance of grain, corn, wine and oil. They did not want for a thing.

Occasionally, they would go to the temple to offer sacrifices that were required and go through the religious motions. However, it did not mean anything. As they continued on this downward spiral, a crisis occurred that captured their attention. A terrible plague of locust swarmed the land and destroyed the crops. The same fields that were at one time overflowing were now empty. The magnitude of the destruction was so devastating that it would take years to recover. Joel came on the scene to speak not only a message of judgment to these wayward people, but also a message of hope. God would restore the years!

God says that I will restore to you the years that you have lost. Before we get into how He is going to restore those years, let us look at how we lost some of those years. What is God talking about when it comes to "years"? God is going to restore our years in two areas. The first relates to the years that you spent outside of His will and not walking in your purpose. You and I have been given a season to fulfill our purpose, and when we miss that season it causes us to feel a sense that we are behind time. Think about all the years that we wasted when we were living in sin. The book of Luke records the account of a young man that wasted all his possessions with prodigal living. When he came to his senses, his father threw a lavish party and restored him (Luke 15:12). We waste money on things that have no eternal value. We waste years by not walking with a sense of purpose in our lives and just living from day to day.

Each day you live without a sense of purpose, you are missing opportunities. God created time so that your purpose would manifest. Maybe like me, you have a story, and although your story may not be the same as mine, if you had any time in your life that was not connected to the Savior, it was probably wasted. We waste years by pursuing things that have nothing to do with our eternal destiny. We lost years by making bad decisions and bad decisions will cost us years. Every decision not only affects you, but also your future. Many decisions of desperation are made to relieve the present without regard to the future. When we get to our future, we have already robbed our future to sustain our past. I am so glad that I serve a God that is able to bend time and restore years. The enemy is a thief and his very nature is to steal.

> *"The thief cometh not, but for to steal, and to kill, and to destroy: I am come that they might have life, and that they might have it more abundantly."* (Jn. 10:10).

Notice the progressive order. It begins with theft and ends with destruction. That is satan's mission. He wants to keep you from the abundant life Jesus came to give you. He wants to steal time from you so your life will not have the impact that it could have. He wants to steal opportunities from you that will keep you from the abundant life. When the enemy steals your time, you have fewer opportunities for your purpose to touch the lives of others.

One of the ways he steals time is through distractions and deception. How is he distracting you? He is distracting you from purpose. When you are distracted, you lose focus with purpose. The enemy sends distractions to divide and divert your attention. When your focus is distracted, you become weak. When you focus is on God's Word and His purpose for your life, you are strong. I have discovered that the enemy does not have to pull you out of church to make you backslide, return to your former ways to make you ineffective and unproductive. If he can just distract you enough, by causing you to miss your season . . . it minimizes the impact your life has on others, and that will be enough for him.

Satan tried to distract Jesus when He was getting ready to go to the cross. Jesus just finished calling Peter, blessed and gave him the keys to the Kingdom (Matt.16:13-20). Peter had just received authority on earth to bind and to loose. Can you imagine all the other apostles looking at him, thinking, *I wish I had said that?* Essentially, Peter was just promoted, and no sooner than his promotion Peter was distracted and allowed satan to use him to hinder Jesus from completing his assignment.

> *"From that time forth began Jesus to shew unto his disciples, how that he must go unto Jerusalem, and suffer many things of the elders and chief priests and scribes, and be killed, and be raised again the third day. Then Peter took him, and began to rebuke him, saying, be it far from thee, Lord: this shall not be unto thee. But he turned, and said unto Peter, Get thee behind me, Satan: thou art an offence unto me: for thou savourest not the things that be of God, but those that be of men."* (Matt. 16:21-24).

There is a very important lesson to learn here. We are not usually distracted at our lowest times—but when we are at a place of promotion—when we are at a place of ease . . . when God has given us an answer or a breakthrough. That is when the enemy tries to snatch what we have just obtained. Do not get distracted at your point of promotion. Thank God, Jesus did not get distracted but He completed His assignment and destroyed the works of the enemy so that we can have abundant life.

The enemy will wait until an opportune time to attack.

> *"It happened in the spring of the year, at the time when kings go out to battle, that David sent Joab and his servants with him, and all Israel; and they destroyed the people of Ammon and besieged Rabbah. But David remained at Jerusalem. Then it happened one evening that David arose from his bed and walked on the roof of the king's house. And from the roof he saw a woman bathing, and the woman was very beautiful to behold. So David sent and inquired about the woman. And*

> *someone said, "Is this not Bathsheba, the daughter of Eliam, the wife of Uriah the Hittite?" Then David sent messengers, and took her; and she came to him, and he lay with her, for she was cleansed from her impurity; and she returned to her house. And the woman conceived; so she sent and told David, and said, "I am with child." (2 Sam. 11:1-5).*

This distraction began when David was in a place he did not belong. When the kings were supposed to be out on the battlefield, King David decided to remain back this time. When you are out of position, you get set up for a distraction that leads to destruction. This distraction ultimately caused a cycle of events to occur that cost a man his life and kept David from fulfilling his heart's desire in building God a house.

Do not allow distractions to rob you from destiny. When God is about to promote you, they enemy always shows up. Recognize the attack as a sign that something great is about to happen. You cannot afford to fall to his deception and lose priceless years or prevent you from your purpose.

3

Season of Restoration

I BELIEVE WE ARE ENTERING INTO a tremendous *season of restoration*. Before Christ returns, I believe we are going to experience a final harvest of restoration so remarkable it will shock the church and overtake the enemy. Restoration is the return of something removed, restoring to its former condition or original state. Restoration means to set in order again. A season of restoration is a time when all things are made right.

In the book of Acts, Peter clearly said there is to be a time when, *"the restoration of all things"* shall take place, a time when all things shall be restored into their perfect state (3:19). Restoration also refers to the rectification of all the disorders of the Fall of Man. As you look into the Scriptures, you will see that *restitution* is a biblical concept closely related to the idea of restoration. Restoration appears to indicate replacement for whatever was taken or destroyed, whereas restitution denotes repayment over and above the actual loss, analogous to what is today called "punitive" damages. (See Exod. 22:1-15; Lev. 6:1-7; Num. 5:5-7). For example, the ancient law found in Exod. 22:1,4 clearly stipulates that anyone who steals an ox or a sheep must pay restitution to the owner of the animal(s). If the thief kills or sells the ox, he is required to pay restitution of five oxen; if he kills or sells the sheep, he is required to pay restitution of four sheep. (See also 2 Sam. 12:6). If, however, the animal has not been harmed and is found safe in the possession of the thief, the culprit is required to pay double. Interestingly enough, if the thief has no means to pay this fine, he is to be sold for his theft.

In Leviticus, it is commanded that if someone robs or cheats a neighbor, that person is to restore the amount in full and add a fifth to it (Lev. 6:1-7). In addition, the guilty party was required to offer a guilt offering. This principle is reflected in the story of Zacchaeus, who, as a tax collector, had cheated and "gouged" the people from whom he had collected the taxes (Luke 19:1-10). After his encounter with Jesus, he voluntarily agreed to give half of his goods to the poor and to restore fourfold to anyone he had defrauded. The principle of restitution is clearly part of this episode, but Zacchaeus went far beyond the requirement of the law in this matter. In most of the New Testament writings, the word group used to designate the idea of restitution or restoration has a rather different meaning, namely that of restoring in the sense of reestablishing.[1]

The Fall of Man affected our spirit, soul, and body, and has now produced disorder and chaos on multiple levels, including our relationships, health, and finances. Jesus Christ came as the Son of Man to rectify these disorders. He is called the last Adam, and He is now the head of a new race that live as people filled with the Spirit of God, *born again*.

When God said, "*I would restore to you the years…*" in Joel chapter 2, He was saying that He was going to restore the years of

---

[1] (See Matt. 17:11; Mark 9:12; Acts 1:6; 3:21) or healing (Matt. 12:13; Mark 3:5; Luke 6:10; Mark 8:25; but cf. Heb. 13:19, where it is somewhat closer to the idea but not in any "legal" sense).

humanity. In other words, God was going to go all the way back to when Adam lost dominion and restore those years to humankind. Jesus, who was the last Adam, was to reveal to us what Adam had the authority and capacity to do in the earth. Every supernatural act, every miracle, every manifestation of power was not done as the Son of God, but rather as the Son of Man. Jesus came to show what Adam had the ability to do. For example, when Jesus fed the multitudes with a few fish, and a couple of loaves of bread, and walked on water . . . He was demonstrating what Adam could have potentially done.

God wants to restore the years by going to go back where Adam forfeited his authority, and lost his capacity—Christ has now come to seek and to save that which was lost (Luke 19:10). Notice it did not say, "*Who* was lost" but rather, "*that which* was lost". When we lost dominion and authority, we also lost time—time we were supposed to be exercising dominion in the earth and extending the boundaries of Eden to cover the whole earth.

This planet has been assigned to man by God. God has given the earth to man to exercise dominion and replicate heaven on earth. *The heaven, even the heavens, are the LORD'S; and the earth hath he given to the children of men."* (Ps. 115:16). Adam was to build a heaven-filled earth. We need more than a revival, a refreshing, and a message that makes us feel good for the moment . . . we need restoration. We are in a time where God is now beginning to orchestrate things to such a degree that He is giving us a moment, a period of time, where we can buy back time.

> *"Repent therefore and be converted, that your sins may be blotted out, so that times of refreshing may come from the presence of the Lord, and that He may send Jesus Christ,*

> *who was preached to you before, whom heaven must receive until the times of restoration of all things, which God has spoken by the mouth of all His holy prophets since the world began."* (Acts 3:19-21).

This season of refreshing only comes when His presence breathes on you and speaks to you. I believe that the Lord takes us through a constant cycle in the process. The Scripture states that heaven must receive or retain Christ until the restitution or restoration of all things. There are things which must be restored before Christ can come back to earth again. Heaven must receive Him "until" the restoration of all things. Do you see how important restoration is?

I want you to see a progressive order in this passage of Scripture. First, there is *repentance*, then *refreshing*, and finally *restoration*. This is the order of the Kingdom. Repentance is always the beginning . . . everything that pertains to the Kingdom begins with repentance.

> *"Now therefore, says the Lord, turn to Me with all your heart, with fasting, with weeping, and with mourning. So rend your heart and not your garments; return to the Lord you God for He is gracious and merciful, slow to anger and of great kindness. And He relents from doing harm who knows if He will turn and relent and leave a blessing behind Him- a grain offering and a drink offering For the Lord your God."* (Joel 2:12-14).

You cannot even begin to experience kingdom realities until you have repented. *Jesus answered and said to him, most assuredly, I say to you, unless one is born again, he cannot see the kingdom of God."* (Jn. 3:3). Repentance then initiates refreshing. That refreshing is replenishing you from the effects that sin had on your life which progresses to restoration. There is no restoration without repentance. Restoration is not automatic; there are some pre-requisites that must be met.

There must first be a returning with our hearts. When our hearts return to God, He will turn, relent, and leave a blessing behind. That blessing left behind was "rain" which is necessary for the wheat, wine, and oil.

> *"When I shut up the heavens so that there is no rain, or command the locust to devour the land, or send pestilence among my people, 14 if my people who are called by my name humble themselves, pray, seek my face, and turn from their wicked ways, then I will hear from heaven, and will forgive their sin and heal their land."* (2 Chron. 7: 13).

When you return to the Lord, God will release the rain of refreshing and the harvest that looked dried up will be reactivated in your life. Repentance is not a one-time event, even though it is initiated by our new birth experience. Repentance, refreshing and restoration is a lifestyle that we must cooperate with. Second, I want you to see that there are "times" of refreshing. There are multiple seasons of refreshing and multiple seasons of restoration.

Once we have come to the place of repentance, then God will begin to release seasons of refreshing. When you have gone through a season of loss, a season of devastation, or stripping, you need to be refreshed. When you have suffered loss, it has the ability to deplete you of strength and energy. Fatigue begins to set in. You can be spiritually drained, emotionally exhausted, and physically weary. When you are worn out, or you have gone through physical and mental exertion you experience reduction in your efficiency. This can take place over a prolonged period. You were designed to be efficient, yet when you have taken a "hit," it is as if the wind is knocked out of you. As a result, you will not be able to accomplish the things that you desire.

Everyone has gone through a season where you have had the wind knocked out of you. It is a place where you need to be reinvigorated. God wants you to be refreshed. You need to be refreshed before God begins to bring new opportunities into your life because He doesn't want you to go into your next season with the wind out of you. When you are fatigued, you are emotionally exhausted.

> *"Have you not known? Have you not heard? The everlasting God, the LORD, the Creator of the ends of the earth, neither faints nor is weary. His understanding is unsearchable He gives power to the weak, and those who have no might He increases strength. Even the youths shall faint and be weary, and the young men shall utterly fall, but those who wait on the Lord shall renew their strength: They shall mount up with wings like eagles, they shall run and not be weary, they shall walk and not faint."* (Isa. 40: 28).

Everyone goes through seasons of fatigue. However, you must learn the art of "waiting on the Lord." You are waiting *on* God, not waiting *for* God. Waiting on the Lord is a picture of a rope entwined around a pole. In other words, when you are waiting on God, you are entwining yourself around him, completely wrapping yourself around him and extracting His strength into your life.

God is committed to your refreshing. God says through Jeremiah, "*I will refresh the weary.*" (Jer. 31:25). You cannot fulfill the potential of your divine assignment without being refreshed. God uses many ways and means to bring refreshing into our lives.

God uses people to bring refreshing to us. God used a man named Onesiphorus to refresh the Apostle Paul. *"The Lord grant mercy to the household of Onesiphorus, for he often refreshed me, and was not ashamed of my chain; but when he arrived in Rome, he sought me out very zealously and found me. The Lord grant to him that he may find mercy from the Lord in that Day—and you know very well how many ways he ministered to me at Ephesus."* (2 Tim. 1:16-18). Yes, the great man of God who wrote the majority of the New Testament needed to be refreshed. This man's assignment was to be an instrument of refreshing to the Apostle. You never get to the point in life that you do not need to be refreshed by somebody. *"A faithful messenger refreshes his masters."* (Prov. 25:13). God will send people into our lives that possess a wonderful gift of encouragement and refreshment. Even if you serve in some type of leadership capacity there are times when you will need to be refreshed by others.

When things are not going the way that you would desire them to go, you will need to be open to people that God will send you just to refresh you. You may be one of those people that God uses to bring refreshing to others. This is not to be taken lightly. Your presence can literally refresh the spirit of another person. There are people that you will meet on a daily basis who at some point will need refreshing in their lives. *"Good news is like cold water to a weary soul."* (Prov. 25:25).

Worship is also a means of refreshing your soul. David's playing refreshed King Saul. By listening to anointed worship music, it releases the presence of God into your life. Listen, there are times when you have taken such a spiritual hit that it is difficult to worship. However, if you can put on a CD, and get around some people that know how to connect with God in worship, you will begin to see that is when the presence of God manifests. That is when peace, joy, and refreshing will come and strengthen you.

God wants your soul to be refreshed. Many do not understand the value and importance of refreshing in the soulish realm. When you experience devastation, it affects your soul—your mind, desires, ambition, passion, and emotions. When swarmed by the cankerworm and palmerworm, your mind (soul) is negatively affected and your emotions are all over the place. If you lose ambition, you lose the desire and passion to achieve something, typically requiring determination and hard work.

God has a purpose for your life. That purpose is going to require ambition, determination, hard work, and diligence. Without ambition, you will not have the fuel to fulfill your divine assignment. One of the first things that God begins to do is refresh you so that you get your ambition back, get your fuel back, and get your emotional energy back.

Restoration is the return of something removed, restoring of something to its former condition. The word implies to set things in order again. When sin entered into the world, death entered, disease entered, poverty entered, and shame entered. Peter clearly says there is to be a time when "the restoration of all things" shall take place, a time when all things are restored to their perfect state. This also refers to the time when Adam walked on the earth. While Adam was in the Garden there was complete order, and harmony. Everything was functioning properly. Adam's relationship with Eve functioned in order as well as his relationship with God. Everything that pertained to Adam functioned as originally intended.

Christ came to restore and give abundant life. The restored life is one that experiences life and life more abundantly. As He moved about on the earth for three and one-half years, He was restoring people's lives, back to where their lives were functioning properly. When Jesus comes into our life, restoration is inevitable.

SEVEN AREAS OF RESTORATION

SOUL

"He restoreth my soul: he leadeth me in the paths of righteousness for his name's sake." (Ps. 23:3).

God wants to restore your soul. Emotions greatly influence how we live our lives. They are a gift from God, provided so we can enjoy life and relate to others, but how we express them determines whether they are beneficial or detrimental. Either we control them or they control us. How many people have damaged emotions brought on by hurt and loss? When a person has damaged and wounded emotions, it can stunt his or her development, growth and enjoyment in life. God wants to bring your emotions back to a place of wholeness. Jesus did not just say "be healed" but he said "be whole." Not only was He healing their physical bodies but he was also healing the part of their soul damaged by the disease, hurt and pain.

JOY

"The joy of the Lord is our strength." (Neh. 8:10).

Joy is consistently one of the marks of a Christian believer. *"Restore unto me the joy of thy salvation; and uphold me with thy free spirit."* (Ps. 51:12). It is a quality, and not simply an emotion, grounded upon God himself and derived from Him. *"Thou wilt shew me the path of life: In thy presence is fulness of joy; at thy right hand there are pleasures for evermore."* (Ps. 16:11). These two work together. If you get in the presence of God, not only will you have joy, but also that joy will be your strength. Life has a way of depleting you of both strength and joy. The enemy tries to keep us out of the presence of God in order so that we will not be able to access God's joy and operate on our own strength. It is amazing what can happen, when a person accesses the presence of God, what it can do to your soul and spirit.

I often say that there is a difference between going to church and entering into His presence. Accessing the presence of God begins by being a person of thanksgiving and praise. Just showing up to church will not do the job. You must learn to cultivate a heart of thanksgiving and praise. *"Enter into his gates with thanksgiving, and into his courts with praise: Be thankful unto him, and bless his name. For the Lord is good; his mercy is everlasting; and his truth endureth to all generations."* (Ps. 100:4-5). When you learn how to be a person of joy, to rejoice in the Lord always, and make it a lifestyle, then your life will be characterized by joy. God can restore your years by restoring joy to you when you previously had years of an unfulfilled life.

TIME

"And I will restore to you the years that the locust hath eaten, the cankerworm, and the caterpillar, and the palmerworm, my great army which I sent among you." (Joel 2:25).

This is the main subject of this book, namely, to have God allow your years restored. I have seen God take what people have lost in years and give them back in months. When God gives something back, it usually does not come back the same way it left. It usually comes back with more.

HEALTH

"For I will restore health unto thee, and I will heal thee of thy wounds, saith the LORD; because they called thee an Outcast, saying, This is Zion, whom no man seeketh after." (Jer. 30:17).

Sickness is one of the effects of sin and the fall. The enemy tries to come against the will of God through attacking your body with sickness. Sickness is not from God. One of the reasons Christ came into the world.

"He that committeth sin is of the devil; for the devil sinneth from the beginning. For this purpose was the Son of God manifested, that he might destroy the works of the devil." (1 Jn. 3:8).

When Jesus walked the face of the earth, he was destroying the works of the devil. One of those works was sickness. Every time Jesus healed someone, He was destroying the works of the devil. You and I are now invited to destroy the works of the devil just as well.

"How God anointed Jesus of Nazareth with the Holy Ghost and with power: who went about doing good, and healing all that were oppressed of the devil; for God was with him." (Acts 10:38)

It is time to get years back that has been robbed from you through sickness.

VISION

"After that he put his hands again upon his eyes, and made him look up: and he was restored, and saw every man clearly." (Mk. 8:25).

Here is another example of God restoring someone's health. God had restored this man's sight. God wants to restore your vision. He wants to restore your dreams. He has a hope and a future for you. Where there is no vision, you perish. (See Prov. 29:18) The enemy wants to steal your future and your dreams. However, Christ came that we might have life more abundantly (John 10:10).

PROPERTY

"Men do not despise a thief, if he steals to satisfy his soul when he is hungry; But if he be found, he shall restore sevenfold; he shall give all the substance of his house." (Prov. 6:30-32).

When the devil stripped Job of his possessions, it appeared that satan finally was able to get to Job. The devil's ploy is to attack us through the materialistic things that we own by stripping us of them. However, God made sure that Job was restored sevenfold.

SELF ESTEEM

"Brethren, if a man be overtaken in a fault, ye which are spiritual, restore such an one in the spirit of meekness; considering thyself, lest thou also be tempted." (Gal. 6:1).

Of all the things the enemy tries to destroy in our lives is our self-esteem. Sin has a way of stripping a person. Paul wrote to believers, not to unbelievers, when he said that if a brother is overtaken in a fault, not to criticize him, but rather to restore him.

There has been a lot of good people that have made bad decisions, and even after repentance, they are criticized harshly, rather than restored. As a result, some have departed the fellowship of believers. This is truly sad, because we are called to restore a believer not tear them down. That is the enemy's job. Our job is to exercise the ministry of reconciliation and restoration. We can help others get their lives back on track by ministering restoration to them.

4

The Harvest Factor

WHEN MINISTERING ON THE topic of time, I generally started by reading the text that states, *"Be glad then ye children of Zion and rejoice in the Lord your God."* (Joel 2:23). To be frank with you, I never really paid that much attention to the context. I guess I was in such in a hurry to get to "my years restored" that I overlooked something's. As I meditated on the context further, I saw how God started by saying, *"Be glad then Children of Zion and rejoice in the Lord your God"* and then concluded the passage, *"My people will never be put to shame."* (Joel 2:26). He does not say that once, but twice! God begins by saying *"Rejoice and be glad."* Have you ever been through a season of loss? It is hard to rejoice during those times. If you have ever been fired, laid off, had a car repossessed, lost a home to foreclosure and gone through a season of destruction. Yet, God says to rejoice and be glad.

He is not saying to rejoice and be glad because it happened. God does not take pleasure when you go through a season of destruction. He does not take pleasure in your losses. That is not what it means. He told them to rejoice because they had just gone through a season of devastation and He was telling them, "praise me in advance because your season of devastation has expired and I am getting ready to bring restoration." It takes faith to praise God in advance. Those who trust God can praise God in advance before they even see the restoration of their losses come into their lives.

When God says to rejoice and be glad, He is commanding us to praise because it has the ability to shift our attitude. The reason is that it takes the focus and attention off us and puts it on Him. Praise is not optional. Praise is a command. God does not say praise me if you have had a good day, or praise me if you feel like it. Praise is not predicated on our emotions. That is why we worship God in spirit and in truth. The thing about praise is that it does something to your spirit. Praise releases joy.

When you have gone through a season of loss, it has a way of depleting your strength. Yet, when you turn your tears to praise, God will release joy in you that is unspeakable and full of glory. One of the ways that you know your season has shifted is when your spirit is filled with joy and laughter. There are different types of laughter when you look at the Word of God. The first laughter is what I call *laughter of unbelief.* In other words, when God speaks something to you that seems so ridiculous, you laugh inside. We probably have all experienced that at one time or another. God speaks something that you think that is too good to be true. Abraham and Sarah both experienced a laugh of unbelief.

> *And God said unto Abraham, As for Sarai thy wife, thou shalt not call her name Sarai, but Sarah shall her name be. 16 And I will bless her, and give thee a son also of her: yea, I will bless her, and she shall be a mother of nations; kings of people shall be of her. 17 Then Abraham fell upon his face, and laughed, and said in his heart, Shall a child be born unto him that is an hundred years old? and shall Sarah, that is ninety years old, bear?* (Gen. 17: 15-17)

Here is Abraham, after he had received a name change from God, he laughed at the idea that this could actually manifest because he and his wife were past the age of having children. They were looking at their natural circumstances. Sarah laughed also.

> *Where is Sarah thy wife? And he said, Behold, in the tent. And he said, I will certainly return unto thee according to the time of life; and, lo, Sarah thy wife shall have a son. And Sarah heard it in the tent door, which was behind him. Now Abraham and Sarah were old and well stricken in age; and it ceased to be with Sarah after the manner of women. Therefore Sarah laughed within herself, saying, After I am waxed old shall I have pleasure, my lord being old also? And the Lord said unto Abraham, Wherefore did Sarah laugh, saying, Shall I of a surety bear a child, which am old? Is anything too hard for the Lord?* (Gen. 18: 9-14)

The key to this type of laughing is that people think that what God had spoken and promised them is too difficult for Him to do.

There is another form of laughter, which is associated with fulfillment of a promise. This is why I call *harvest laughter*. In other words, when God performs and does what He said He was going to do, there will be an expression of joy that will be so great that it will find expression through laughter. "*And Abraham was an hundred years old, when his son Isaac was born unto him. 6 And Sarah said, God hath made me to laugh, so that all that hear will laugh with me.*" (Gen. 21:5-6).   When you begin to move into a season of your harvest, there will be a laughter and joy that comes with it. When all you went through is past and now you are in your harvest season, there is such a joy and laughter. God was able to take Sarah's impossibility and cause her to conceive and He fulfilled what He said He was going to do.

There is another form of laughter, which is the *laughter of victory*. When you can laugh about the things that used to make you cry, you have just crossed over the threshold of victory. Laughter is a signal to the enemy that his plans are in vain.

> "*Why do the heathen rage, And the people imagine a vain thing? The kings of the earth set themselves, And the rulers take counsel together, Against the Lord, and against his anointed, saying, Let us break their bands asunder, And cast away their cords from us. He that sitteth in the heavens shall laugh: The Lord shall have them in derision.*" (Ps. 2:1-4).

What God is saying in this passage is that while the rulers are setting themselves against His anointed and plotting against His anointed, He is sitting in heaven and laughing because all of their energy and plotting is going to come to nothing. It is going to be in vain. "*The wicked plotteth against the just, And gnasheth upon him with his teeth. The Lord shall laugh at him: For he seeth that his day is coming.*" (Ps. 37:12-13). We can get to that place where whatever the enemy has been plotting against you will come to nil. You can come into the place of agreement with God and if God is laughing at all the plans the enemy is trying to devise against you, you can laugh also. You can laugh because you know that no weapon that is formed against you will prosper (Is. 54: 17).

God had told the children of Israel to rejoice in advance because He was getting ready to bring them restoration. Look what happens when God begins to turn your captivity around.

> "*When the Lord turned again the captivity of Zion, We were like them that dream. Then was our mouth was filled with laughter, And our tongue with singing: Then said they among the heathen, The Lord hath done great things for them. The Lord hath done great things for us; Whereof we are glad. Turn again our captivity, O Lord, As the streams*

in the south. They that sow in tears shall reap in joy. He that goeth forth and weepeth, bearing precious seed, shall doubtlesss come again with rejoicing, bringing his sheaves with him." (Ps. 124).

When God turned their captivity, they felt as if they were dreaming. God filled their mouths with laughter and their tongues with singing. God will turn your tears to laughter. Then they said, the Lord has done great things for them. They changed what they said. When God turns your captivity, when you recover your seasons, you will also begin to say along with them, "The Lord has done great things for me!" You went out weeping, but you came back rejoicing. Is that not just like our God? Laughter then marks the end of a season of loss and initiates the season of restoration.

5

Unexpected Harvest

WE HAVE DISCOVERED THAT IT is the will of God to bring restoration. He wants you restored in every area of your life. He is invested in restoring years that you have missed. This is one of the greatest things about our salvation. God can make seasons up to us that we forfeited before coming to know Him. As we have previously established, God works in seasons and cycles. If we missed out with seasons in our lives, God is able to make it up and able to redeem time.

When the prophet Joel proclaimed his warning, recorded in chapter 2, historically, it was during a time when Israel rebelled against God. Now, in order to understand his message, we must see the comparison between the devastation from the insects that destroyed the crops and judgment of God against sin. In addition, to comprehend Joel's message, we need to consider the cycles of planting, sowing and harvesting crops. In order to retrieve a harvest, you are going to need rain. If there were no rain, then there would be no harvest, which would cause their economy to collapse. If there was plenty of rain, it produced a greater harvest that greatly affected their economy.

In the pursuit of redeeming time, rain is essential to your harvest—no rain—no harvest. Likewise, if there is little rain—little harvest, or much rain—much harvest. In other words, the amount of rain is an indicator to the harvest in your life. If there is plenty of rainfall, your financial situation changes dramatically. Often, when people have problems monetarily they immediately plant seed (invest the resources in good soil). Yet, if there is no rain, your seed is wasted. Imagine seed that you have sown in the past and are yet to germinate because there was no rain. There is nothing wrong with the seed. You just lack the rainfall. Rain also symbolizes opportunities.

You have seed (invaluable resources) in you. You have buried talents, gifts, and strengths that if given the right opportunity can greatly change your life. How many people have giftings and buried talents but no opportunities to release them? I believe that God has placed seed of potential and destiny on the inside of you and when it begins to rain opportunities in your life, it will produce an enormous harvest.

> *"For the land which you go to possess is not like the land of Egypt from which you have come, where you sowed your seed and watered it by foot, as a vegetable garden; but the land which you cross over to possess is a land of hills and valleys, which drinks water from the rain of heaven, a land for which the Lord your God cares; the eyes of the Lord your God are always on it, from the beginning of the year to the very end of the year. And it shall be that if you earnestly obey My commandments which I command you today, to love the Lord your God and serve Him with all your heart and with all your soul, then I will give you the rain for your land in its season, the early rain and the latter rain, that you may gather in your grain, your new wine, and your oil. And I will send grass in your fields for your livestock, that you may eat and be filled."* (Deut.11:10-15)

God says in the above passage that the land He was about to give them is not like the land they came out of. Egypt was a low flat land, not watered by rain, but rather by the Nile River. They developed irrigation systems in order to water the land. This took a great deal of energy, work, and labor. The location God was giving to them was their destiny land—a land with hills and valleys. In other words, it had a built-in irrigation system, one that He designed especially for them. Think of it, He already constructed a land that would be conducive for their harvest. The land that God was going to giving them drew in the water without any need of physical labor. Because of the way the land was designed, the rain came TO them! The rain was absorbed into the earth, and was able to bring forth a superior harvest.

Listen to what the writer of Hebrews states, *"For the earth which drinketh in the rain that cometh oft upon it, and bringeth forth herbs meet for them by whom it is dressed, receiveth the blessing from God."* (Heb. 6:7). God's Word is saying that the earth, which drinks in the rain, brings forth fruitfulness for the person whom it is prepared and that person receives the blessing from the Lord. Therefore, rain is vitally important to your harvest. We must learn that if we want God to restore us, we must properly position ourselves to receive the blessing of the Lord.

We need to learn how to drink in the rain (the presence of God). We need to get soaked with God's presence. There are times when we need to experience His company in such a way that we are totally soaked and absorbed with the glory of God. This can occur in times of prayer or worship. We need to learn how to get comfortable with just getting soaked. Much of our prayer and worship is very activity oriented. However, there are times when you need to let God soak you with His glory and goodness. The writer did not just say that the earth was soaked once, but rather he states "oft," meaning constantly, frequently, time after time. This cannot just be an occasional experience, but it must become a lifestyle.

The Scripture then states that once the earth is soaked and experiences the rain that it bears, brings forth and produces for the one who cultivates it. The earth was made to cooperate with you. Once the rain falls, it brings forth your increase. Once the rain falls, it waters what has already been sown. The water connects with the seed that causes it to germinate then all you have to do is cultivate, or manage your increase.

> *"For He has given you the former rain faithfully, and He will cause to come down for you the former rain, in the first month."* (Joel 2:23).

In Israel, there were two different rainy seasons. The *former* rain softened the soil for planting winter wheat and the *latter* rain, which fell usually six months later, which caused the grain to swell, and ensured a good harvest. If the rains failed, the crops would not grow. If there were little rain, there would be little harvest. For every harvest, there is a rain linked to the harvest. When God told them He was going to give them the years back, He was not just talking about time, but rather He was going to give them back all of the previous harvests' that were connected to the time. In other words, think where your life would be right now if you had not missed previous opportunities ten, fifteen, twenty, thirty, or even forty years ago.

Personally, I do not want to go back forty years to experience my teenage years again. However, if I could go back and retrieve opportunities back again that I missed in my 20's and 30's, I would probably be at a different place in my life now. However, we cannot continue to live in a place called "regret." We must forget those things, which are behind us and reach for those things, which are before us. God has the capacity to cause our lives to be affected and accelerated in such a way that we end up being where we would have been if we would have passed through all of the opportunities that we missed out on. *God is a time bender.* What do I mean by that? Let me paint a picture for you.

Let me illustrate, say that I take a man's belt, a big belt and hold the belt in both of my hands. One part of the belt is in my left hand, the other part is in my right hand, and I stretch the belt out so that it is tight. Say that one end of the belt signifies the point of your birth and the other end of the belt signifies your death, obviously, we do not exactly know when that will be. However, for the sake of teaching, now take your age and find out where you fit in that belt. If you are forty or fifty, you are probably closer to the middle of the belt than a person who just turned 10. Now, let us say that you are fifty and you find yourself close to the middle of the belt line, and you put your finger there. Then all of the belt to the left of your hand would be all those years of harvests that you had forfeited. That may be many years. You look the other direction and you only have so many years to try to play "catch up" with all of your missed opportunities.

I do not have another fifty years to make up for the last fifty years of my life, but this is the way many people think. The older you get, you are less likely to take risks to help you be caught up. The reason for this is that you cannot afford to be risky because if you make a bad decision again it could cost you years and money that you may not have time to make up if you lose it again. At least when you were younger, you had time on your side and could afford to be more uncertain in your career and money, but the older you get, you cannot afford to be as chancy. However, in this illustration there is a discrepancy. When I hold out the belt—it represents time as being linear. That is how we view time. We view it as beginning to the end. However, in the Hebrew mindset time is not linear but circular. Time means that the end is wedged into the beginning and the beginning is wedged in the end. When the end is wedged in the beginning and the beginning is wedged into the end, you cannot tell where the beginning begins nor the end ends—so it is with God. This is why Christ was the lamb slain from the beginning of the world (Rev. 13:8).

Now back to my illustration with the belt. Say I took that one end of belt and bent it so that the left side looped over until it connected with right side so you have a circular piece of leather. This is what God can do. He can bend time, so that what was lost in your past you can recover in the future. Our God is awesome. So while you are moving forward into your tomorrow's opportunities, then those missed opportunities are "bent" so that they will meet you there as well.

Now remember there were two different rains in Israel. The first rain was also called the *rain of vindication*. This is necessary for your life. The first rain softened and prepared the soil. When we have forfeited harvests' because of poor decision making, we have missed out on future opportunities. We create negative history in our lives. You may have had a bad first marriage that is keeping you from entering into a new relationship. You may have accumulated negative credit history that is hindering you now for new opportunities. Yet, this first rain is a rain of vindication. The rain of vindication erases the shame of your devastation. (We will go further into understanding shame later in the book).

To vindicate someone is to clear a person of shame, blame, and guilt. This rain is a cleansing rain. This represents the times of refreshing that comes from God's presence. God wants to cleanse you, vindicate you, clear you, and give you a fresh start in life. It is not that we are trying to pass off the blame to someone else, but rather, we are accepting responsibility for the decisions we have made that were not in agreement with God's Word. Since we were not in agreement with God's will and plan, we find ourselves in a position of experiencing loss. When a person repents to God and confesses his sin, the Word of God will open the heavens and send the rain.

> *"When I shut up heaven and there is no rain, or command the locust to devour the land, or send pestilence among my people, if my people who are called by My name will humble themselves and pray and seek my face, and turn from their wicked ways, then I will hear from heaven, and forgive their sin, and heal their land."* (2 Chron. 7: 13-14).

God says that he has been consistent in sending the former and the latter rain in previous years of their lives. Now that they find themselves is a season of devastation, they have gone years without rain because of disobedience. They lost years of opportunities, years of harvest. However, when they repent, the Lord says that He is going to do something supernatural in their lives. He is going to bring the former rain and the latter rain in the first month. These two rainy seasons were six months apart. Yet, God is going to release it in the first month. I want you to understand fully the impact of this verse. Remember, for every raining season, there is a harvest. These two rains represented two different seasons.

God is not going to pull the former into the latter, nor is He going to pull the latter into the former. God is going to actually combine the two different seasons, and create a season that did not exist before. When God combines these two seasons, it releases an exponential increase in your life. This season is created to give you such a harvest that your threshing floors are going to be full of wheat and your barns are going to overflow with new wine and oil. This is a brand new season. This is an unexpected harvest. This season that God created never existed before. When God gets ready to bring full restoration to your life, He has a way of creating a season for you that never existed before. This newly created season is characterized by overflow and abundance.

When is God going to do this? He is going to do it in the first month. The first month of the Hebrew people was between March and April in our calendar. It was during Passover. God was going to pull two different seasons together into one season. In other words, what should have taken you at least six months to get to you will overtake you in the next 30 days.

What you thought would take six months to manifest in your life, can manifest in the next 30 days. I began to experience this for myself personally. I was in a serious financial famine. I had to work multiple jobs just to make ends meet and it still did not seem like enough. When I began to get the revelation of this, something took place in my life that has forever changed me. My income over a six-month period, with the total of all of my jobs, had been condensed into a 30-day period. In other words, what I was making over a six-month period was now manifesting in one month. Imagine if God was to release such a breakthrough in your life, that what you make financially over the next six months will be your new monthly income. Imagine the doors that would open in your life over the course of the next six months—if they were to open over your life in the next 30 days. How would you respond? This is why God said in the beginning of the passage. *"Be glad then ye children of Zion and rejoice in the Lord your God."* (Joel 2:23).

It is time to rejoice. God is going to create a season that is going to blow your mind! Remember, I told you that God has the ability to "bend time." All the previous opportunities you missed out before, He will "bend" to meet you in the future. That means that the harvest connected to your missed seasons, you will walk into. While you are walking into the harvest of your tomorrows, gathering the harvest of your tomorrows, enjoying the harvest of your tomorrows, you will look over your should and there will be another rain coming- that harvest from all of your previous missed opportunities. This is what I believe that the prophet Elijah heard when he stated, "I hear the sound of abundance of rain!"

God has a season for you that the enemy cannot touch. God has a season for you that you have not even messed up yet. God has a season marked and set aside. It is a set harvest waiting on you. This newly created season by God will yield double for your life. You will be gleaning the harvest of your previous missed opportunities as well as gleaning from your harvest of future opportunities. When you step into your harvest, you will begin to move in double. The enemy has been trying to steal your harvest. He comes to steal, kill, and to destroy. However, the Word of God states, *"If the thief be found, he shall pay double."* (Exod. 22:7).

Over 2,000 years ago, the thief was found and apprehended. Christ conquered the enemy. He exposed satan's plans and overcame him. Now, we are going to be recipients of double. Satan tried to bring shame into our lives through lies, deception and pain.

"Instead of your shame you shall have double honor, and instead of confusion they shall rejoice in their portion.

> *Therefore in their land they shall possess double; Everlasting joy shall be theirs."* (Isa. 61:7).

It is time for you to possess double. What you missed out previously will be returned double. This is how you are going to make up for lost time. You are going to get double. What should have taken years to get to you will be coming to show quicker than you imagined. In this way, you will leave no harvest behind. The harvest that you felt you missed out on would meet you in your personal "first month." It is time for you to move into the rainiest season of your life. It is time to get your years back.

6

A Healthy Soul

THE ENEMY WANTS TO EAT away at your harvest. He has no desire for you to increase. He will come at you from multiple angles. He will do anything he can to stop you from moving into your harvest. God mentions four different agents of devastation in Joel 2. He talks about the locust, the cankerworm, the caterpillar, and the palmerworm. Not just one insect came to destroy the harvest. There were four.

One thing I discovered as I studied this passage of Scripture was, each insect ate a different part of the plant of their harvest. These insects also had a persistence that demonstrated their ability to survive under the most difficult conditions. They were also characterized by their ability to move about. They also did not come all at once. They were released at different intervals. The first insect mentioned is the locust. The primary way the locust consumed the crop would be by removing the leaves of the wheat to where it was stripped bare. The ordinary Syrian locust resembles the grasshopper, but is larger and more destructive. The legs and thighs of these insects are so powerful that they can leap to a height of two hundred times the length of their bodies. When so raised, they spread their wings and fly so close together as to appear like one compact moving mass.

Whatever the first locust left behind then came the second, the cankerworm. The cankerworm did not use the same method of destroying the crops as the locust. It would destroy the crops by using its teeth to chew the stalks of grain. This would injure the crop by making deep incisions into the stalks of the grain. Whatever the first and second worms left behind the third insect, the caterpillar, entered through massive invasion and destroyed by swarming. This insect would move about in a hopping manner very randomly in a very confusing way almost without any type of order.

Finally, after all three worms came in, whatever remained, the last insect, the palmerworm, which attacked the harvest by swarming. The palmerworm was unique in the fact of that it was a very migratory insect. It is called a palmerworm because it would wander and travel likes a pilgrim. This worm would travel in bands and thus producing an overwhelming effect.

These all came at different times and in different ways as four agents of devastation that destroyed their harvest. We are going to see the significance of these four agents of devastation and the effect that they have on our lives. There is a connection to your harvest and your soul. The health of your soul is related to your harvest. Your ability to prosper and advance in life is directly tied to the health of your soul. The Apostle John writes, *"Beloved, I wish above all things, that thou mayest prosper and be in health, even as thy soul prospereth."* (3 John 2).

The Apostle John is writing to a man name Gaius. This was John's desire and prayer for him. We know from other writings from John that he was a man of prayer. John was very confident in his prayer that he would offer up to God. John would not pray anything apart from the will of God.

> "And this is the confidence that we have in him, that, if we ask any thing according to his will, he heareth us: And if we know that he hears us, whatsoever we ask, we know that we have the petitions that we desired of him." (1 John 5:14).

John had absolute confidence that when he prayed, God heard him. It is good to know that when you pray, God is not just listening to you but you are being heard of God. Not everyone has that type of confidence. God wants you to have this type of confidence when you go into prayer as John did. How did John get this confidence? Where did it come from? His confidence that he was heard came from praying according to the will of God. How do you pray in accordance to the will of God? You look to the Word of God. The Word of God is the will of God. God's will for your life is revealed through the Word. So, if you discover something in the Word that you desire, then that is the will of God. When you go to God with what He has already said, then you can have absolute confidence that you will be heard. This is how you have the same confidence that John had when he prayer.

John prayed that Gaius would prosper and be in health even as, or in same proportion to his soul prospering. Your soul has a lot to do with you prospering. If you want to prosper then you are going to need doors of opportunity to open for you. If you have missed opportunities, or have experienced any type of loss, then you are going to need to recover. Man is a tripartite being. You are a spirit, you live in a body, and you have a soul.

> "And the very God of peace sanctify you wholly, and I pray God your whole spirit and soul and body be preserved blameless unto the coming of our Lord Jesus Christ". (1Thess. 5:23).

The soul comprises of your mind, will, and emotions. Your mind is the part of you that is the seat of your thought life. Your thought life is extremely important because as a man thinks in his heart so is he. You are what you think about most of the time. Your life is a direct reflection of your thought life. Every thought is a seed that produces some kind of a harvest. Negative thoughts will produce a negative harvest. Positive thoughts will produce a positive harvest. In your soul also lies the seat of your will. God has given every man a free will. He has the capacity to make decisions. This is part of what it means to be in the image and likeness of God. Your will is where you decide. This is where you make your decisions. The decisions we make should be based and grounded on God's word. However, many times we end up making decisions based on our own limited understanding.

> *"Trust in the Lord with thine heart, and lean not unto thine own understanding. In all thy ways acknowledge him and he shall direct thy paths."* (Prov. 3:5).

Daily decisions determine destiny. Life is a series of decisions. To have a healthy soul speaks of your ability to make quality and godly decisions.

Finally, the last part of your soul is the seat of your emotions. Your emotions deal with how you feel at any particular moment. This is where you experience happiness, joy, depression, and anxiety. God's people are not to be led or make decisions based on their emotions. The reason is that your emotions are like the weather. It is subject to change at any moment. *"For we walk by faith and not by sight."* (2 Cor. 5:17).

Your emotions are a very large makeup of who you are. Emotions have a great impact on your life. They can affect your life for either good or bad. Unfortunately, many people live out of the arena of their emotions. We will all experience both positive and negative emotions, yet God does not want our lives to be governed by our emotions. God wants your soul and emotions to be stable and healthy. When you are emotionally healthy, you will not be making decisions based on how you feel, but rather on the word of God.

It is important for your soul to be healed and healthy because if your soul is not whole, and you still have damaged emotions from previous losses, then when new doors of opportunity open up, you may sabotage them. If your soul is not whole, it affects your decision making ability and you may second guess yourself more than usual. If your soul is not whole, how you interact with people will be affected. When you have a healthy soul, you will be in position to walk through the doors of opportunities that God opens up for you.

If the enemy wants to destroy your harvest, he is going to attack your soul. He is going to come after your thought life, your decision making capacity and your emotional life. If your soul is whole, then you will be making healthy choices and decisions. Your emotional life will be healthy and your thought life will be in agreement with the Word of God. God wants you to prosper in the same level as your soul prospers. If you focus on getting your soul whole, then you will begin to see that you will attract new opportunities in your life. Now, we will see how these four agents of devastation will try to plague your soul and keep you from experiencing your harvest. Once you begin to see this, you will also be able to thwart any future attempts from the enemy to attack your soul.

Remember that I shared with you that there were four agents of devastation, the locust, the cankerworm, the caterpillar, and the palmerworm. Each worm attacked different parts of the harvest and did so at different times. These insects attacked the harvest. As a result, years were lost. The years that were lost were connected to their harvest. These insects now represent four ways that your soul is attacked. The health of your soul is connected to your harvest. The way that the insects attacked the harvest was through stripping, cutting, swarming, and hopping. Each of these has a profound impact on your soul.

The first locust devoured the harvest by a stripping effect. When you experience loss of missed opportunities one of the first things that is impacted is that your confidence and self-esteem is stripped. Self-confidence is extremely important in almost every aspect of our lives, yet so many people struggle to find it. People who lack self-confidence can find it difficult to become successful. Low self-confidence can be self-destructive and it often manifests itself as negativity. Self-confident people are generally more positive and believe in themselves and their abilities.

Two main things contribute to self-confidence, self-efficacy and self-esteem. We gain a sense of self-efficacy when we see ourselves mastering skills and achieving goals that matter in our lives. When you are in a season of loss, it is easy for your confidence to be shaken. You begin to question your decisions, beliefs, and strategies. Self-efficacy is the type of confidence that leads people to accept difficult challenges and persist in the face of setbacks. Self-esteem comes from the sense of feeling competent at what we do, and that we can succeed when we put our minds to it. Your confidence will begin to come back once you begin to experience some successes in your life. *"Cast not away therefore your confidence, which hath great recompence of reward."* (Heb. 10:35).

This rebuilding is not a one-time event, but rather a process. I had to go through this process myself. After having gone through and experiencing setbacks in my life, my confidence was extremely shaken to the point where I did not want to step out and try anything new in order to avoid the pain of a setback. This emotional paralysis had me locked up for years. I had finally come across someone who saw me differently than I saw myself. It is amazing that when you go through a loss in your life, your identity will begin to be fashioned based on what you had experienced. Just because you failed at something, does not mean you are a failure. He saw me for who I could become. One thing that stood out that he said to me was, "All you need is one win under your belt to turn this around." One victory, one win is all you need to begin to rebuild your self-confidence. One win breaks a losing streak.

Consequently, every winning streak begins with one win. The confidence that you will begin to regain in your life from one victory will begin to create a momentum in your life that will be unstoppable. Let me share with you a key to setting yourself up for a win. Start with an easy success. What do I mean? Let me give you an example. When I was in my younger years, I used to play football. Many times after you have learned how the offense works and how the defense works, you have all of the systems in place for the game.

We would call a scrimmage before we set out for the regular season. Sometimes, in the scrimmage we would play the second stringers. We would not play a team that would put our players in physical jeopardy but we wanted to build our confidence. There are times you need to set yourself up for an easy win. Confidence does not discriminate between an easy victory and a difficult victory. Confidence is confidence and even if it is a small victory, you will begin to put confidence back into your game. Eventually, with enough wins, you will begin to build up momentum in your life that will cause you to face the most difficult circumstances with new boldness and success. Start by setting goals that are not so insurmountable that you are defeated even before you get started. Once self-confidence is back in your life, no one will be able to take it away from you.

> *"Being confident of this very thing, that he which hath begun a good work in you will perform it until the day of Jesus Christ."* (Phil. 1:6).

There is reward to you having confidence. When your confidence is shaken and you are not moving in confidence you end up defaulting on the reward. *"In whom we have boldness and access with confidence through faith in Him."* (Eph. 3:12). When we lack confidence, it affects how we approach God. We do not usually come to him in faith. Our access is limited, not because God has limited it, but because we lack confidence in approaching God, and we come to God in uncertainty rather than boldness and assurance. God wants us to be people of confidence. First, He wants you to be confidence in your relationship with Him. The enemy wants to destroy your confidence. When you are moving in confidence, your faith is strong, and you are unstoppable. God also wants you to have confidence in your prayer life.

> *"And this is the confidence that we have in him, that, if we ask any thing according to his will, he heareth us: And if we know that he hears us, whatsoever we ask, we know that we have the petitions that we desired of him."* (1 Jn. 5:14-15).

You can see that confidence is even important in your prayer life. God wants you to come boldly before the throne of grace. He wants us to approach Him confidently. He states that this is the confidence we have in Him, that if we ask anything according to His will He hears us. Have confidence in God's Word. God's word will work in your life. God is going to finish what He has started in you. Your confidence is in God. Regardless of what your situation has been saying, you need to stand and be confident that God has too much invested in you to let you lose.

The second insect was the cankerworm. The cankerworm destroyed the crops by cutting and making incisions on the stalks of what was left over after the locust. We have all gone through seasons in our lives where we have experienced the pain of being cut. Not cut physically but rather wounded emotionally. We can have our heart wounded so many different ways. It can be cut by betrayal, or even by words that people say. Words can cut. Words can wound a person's soul.

"But the tongue can no man tame; it is an unruly evil, full of deadly poison." (James 3:8).

Words have power and influence our lives. Negative words spoken over you can have a negative impact on your soul. Words spoken by people you do not know will not have an impact on your life as much as the words spoken to you by people that are close to you, either by a loved one, a teacher, a coach, a friend, or a schoolmate. Negative words spoken over your life contain a poison designed to wound and strip you down of self-esteem, confidence and self-worth. You may have forgotten what had been said to you, but the residue still remains in you and has negatively impacted your soul. If those wounding words go through your life unchecked, you end up coming into an agreement with them and they will have a power over you that will reshape your emotions, thoughts, and behaviors.

Negative words must be dealt with. If you do not deal with them, they will end up destroying your harvest. One of the ways negative words destroy your harvest is how words affect your confidence and self-esteem. Confidence is critical in you securing your harvest and walking through new doors of opportunity. Words affect your perception. When your perception is not in line with truth, you end up constructing a false belief system, and talk yourself out of your harvest.

You will find an example of this in the book of Numbers, chapter 13. God told the children of Israel that He had given them the land of promise. God told Moses to send men that they may search the land. Moses told them to survey the land and also to bring back fruit of the land. These men had brought back fruit from the land. When they returned, they said, "It surely flows with milk and honey, and here is the fruit of the land." In other words, it is just as God said. Then they added their own opinion by using one word that shifted everything, "nevertheless." They said "nevertheless," the people in that city are strong, the walls are fortified, and the men are huge.

These men were now releasing negative words that caused the people to get into an uproar to the point that Caleb had to still the people. Caleb said, "Let us go at once." The people responded by saying, "We are not able to go up for they are stronger than we are." Do you think God knew exactly how strong these men were before He told them to go up? Their words caused a whole generation to miss out their harvest, promise and destiny. When negative words are affirmed, you end up disqualifying yourself from future opportunities.

How do we heal from words spoken over us? First, you need to operate in forgiveness. Jesus had many negative, hurtful words spoken concerning Him. Yet, he never opened his mouth and retaliated. Forgiveness is the first step in healing from negative words. Forgive those that spoke those words of negativity over your life. Forgiveness frees you so that you can be healed and move forward. Second, you need to renounce those words that have wounded you.

> "No weapon formed against thee shall prosper; and every tongue that shall rise against thee in judgment thou shalt condemn. This is the heritage of the servants of the Lord, and their righteousness is of me, saith the Lord." (Isa. 54:17).

Negative words are arrows filled with poison to wound your heart. You have the power to condemn the effect of those words. God says, "YOU SHALL CONDEMN." God is not going to do it for you. You have to renounce those words that have negatively affected you and then reaffirm God's truth in your heart and mind. Negative words designed to strip you of your identity in Him. God said that our righteousness is because of Him. No matter what anyone says, you are the righteousness of God in Him.

> "For He hath made him to be sin for us, who knew no sin; that we might be made the righteousness of God in him." (2 Cor. 5:21)

You must replace negative words that wounded you with God's Word of truth. Say what God has said about you and not what others have said about you. When you begin to say what God says about you, you will begin to see that you will become a magnet of favor.

If you truly believe God to give you new and exciting opportunities, you must be built up in your inner man and soul.

You must be like Joshua and Caleb when they said, "we are well able." You are well able. You have the ability of God working in you. You can do all things through Christ Jesus. You have the mind of Christ. You are more than a conqueror. Make affirmations of who you are. Once you begin to do that, your self-esteem will begin to soar. Then, when God begins to present new opportunities in your life there will be a favor upon you that you have an expectation of walking through that door. The only way that you can prove the will of God is with a renewed mind. You must have your mind renewed by the Word of God. When you mind is renewed, your life will be transformed. Say what you want to see rather than what you see. Say the same thing that God says.

"Death and Life are in the power of the tongue." (Prov. 18: 21)

Your tongue has power. It can determine the direction of your life. This principle is true not only for believers but also for unbelievers. However, God's word has a power and authority that is supreme to all other words. When God's people say what God's word says, there is a power that is released that an unbeliever does not have access to. It is the miraculous explosive power of the *rhema* word of God.

The third locust invaded the crop by the form of swarming. You may wonder how this relates to your soul. This is when a person is feeling overwhelmed. You get to the point where you just cannot take anymore. In our soul, we have an emotional capacity. There are times when your soul gets to the point where you are feeling overwhelmed. You have just hit your limit. We are not designed to carry negative emotions to this degree. This is why your body starts to shut down in many ways. This is when you begin to feel heaviness, fatigue, bitter, resentful, and irritable. These negative emotions will begin to affect your heart as well as your social interaction with people. If you are experiencing these things, you will end up repelling any future opportunities that may present themselves to you. People end up becoming self-absorbed with their own problems. These emotions are real, and they have a real impact on your soul. God's word gives a remedy for being healed in this area and experiencing the peace of God.

"Casting all your care upon Him, for He cares for you." (1 Peter 5:7).

God cares about what you care about. You must cast your cares upon Him. What are you caring about that is causing you to feel overwhelmed? To cast your cares literally means to roll it over to him. He can carry you. He can carry what you are trying to carry. When you roll it over to him, make sure you don't pick it back up again. When you roll your concerns to the Lord, you are expressing your faith in Him.

"Be careful for nothing; but in everything by prayer and supplication with thanksgiving let your requests be made known unto God. And the peace of God that passeth all understanding shall keep your hearts and minds through Christ Jesus." (Phil. 4:6-7).

The Apostle Paul is saying do not get anxious for anything. Anxiousness is an indication that you have not rolled your cares upon the Lord. People experience anxiety for many different reasons. Typically, they all experience some type of unease, worry, nervousness about an imminent event of which there is an uncertain outcome. You cannot have worry and the peace of God at the same time. When you pray and release those things, which you are concerned about, God, will release His peace into your life.

I like how the Scriptures say that the peace of God that passes all understanding. There is a dimension of peace that transcends anything we have ever known, and that can be experienced while you are facing your problems. In the book of Mark, chapter four, there is an account where Jesus has just finished telling his disciples a parable about the sower and the seed. After He had finished the parable, he tells them to go to the other side. Jesus goes to the lower part of the ship. In the midst of them going to the other side, a storm arises. They then proceeded to wake Jesus from his sleep and said to him, *"Carest thou not that we perish?"* (Mark 4: 38)

Jesus arose and rebuked the wind and said to the sea, *"Peace be still,"* and the wind ceased and there was a great calm. Jesus was not anxious in the midst of the storm. He already knew that the storm was going to come. I have often said that the reason that Jesus was able to sleep through the storm is that the dimension that He lives in is one where storms do not exist. He had a peace that transcended all understanding.

The Apostle Paul then states that the peace that transcends all understanding will keep your hearts and minds in Christ Jesus. The word "keep" means to be a watcher in advance, i.e. to mount guard as a sentinel (post spies at gates); fig. to hem in, and protect. That peace will literally act as a sentinel or guard and protect your mind, heart and soul. Peace guards by keeping anxieties from your heart, which in turn affects your choices, and your mind, including its attitudes, both of which are part of your soul.

I have previously talked about how these locusts also represent ways that our soul is affected. The last locust came through the harvest by way of a hopping effect. You may wonder how this relates to the soul, especially in relation to redeeming time and lost opportunities. When the soul has gone through the losses of missed opportunities and loss of time, one of the things that plagues the soul the most is the sense of confusion. The hopping affect represents confusion. It is not necessarily the sense of confusion between making decisions, but rather the sense of bewilderment of what just took place. The enemy tries to keep God's people in a sense of confusion. When we are in confusion, our soul is not functioning the way that it should. Our decisions are not sound. Our emotions are all over the place. Our sense of timing is off. Our sense of direction is misplaced. When you are in confusion, there is a sense of bewilderment. God is not the author of confusion. One of the words that help to explain confusions is uncertainty. God does not want us living in a place of uncertainty.

"The steps of a righteous man are ordered by the Lord, and He delights in his way." (Ps.37:23).

God wants your steps ordered. A step ordered by God is an established step. When God orders our steps, it brings stability and not uncertainty. I have found that people get off track because they end up making decisions as a reaction to a life interruption. Often, when something has happened in our lives, we do not think things through and as a result, we make decisions. These rash decisions are nothing more than a quick reaction to the pressure. If you really think about it, the majority of decisions you made that did not turn out right was not a result of getting council from God. Most of the time that we made bad decisions was a result of feeling under pressure and then reacting to alleviate that pressure.

However, God is merciful. He is able to redeem even your bad decisions. If you have gone through a situation and there is a sense of confusion in your soul, the first thing to do is to learn how to quiet your soul. *"Surely, I have calmed and quieted my soul."* (Ps.

131:2). This takes great discipline. Your mind may be racing and your emotions may be all over the place. However, if you are going to hear from God to have your next step be one of certainty and success, you are going to have to quiet your soul so that you hear clearly from God. When God speaks to you and guides you, He is going to guide you and speak to you through your inner man; your spirit.

> *"The spirit of a man is the candle of the Lord, searching all the inward parts of the belly."* (Prov. 20:27).

If your soul is in an uproar, it is difficult to hear in your spirit. This is why you have to calm and quiet your soul, which includes your mind, will, and emotions. Quieting your soul is best accomplished through prayer and meditation. As you enter into prayer, you must quiet your soul. Focusing on the greatness of God, the attributes of God and the Word of God brings the mind, emotions, and will into a place of alignment. This alignment will allow you to hear clearly and make decisions based on the Word of God. God will speak to your spirit through His Word.

Anytime we incur a loss in our lives, especially if it is a result of sin or disobedience, shame enters into our soul. Shame is associated with lack, loss and devastation. The root of the word shame means, "to cover." Shame is a sense of consciousness that is associated with dishonor, disgrace, inadequacy, and humiliation. When you have experienced failure or disappointment, your soul and mind may experience disgrace, dishonor, inadequacy and humiliation. Shame is a result of your harvest being devastated. Shame was the result when Adam and Eve had sinned against God; they were naked and ashamed. Before the fall, Adam and Eve were naked and were not ashamed. They were also crowned with the glory and honor of God.

"What is man that thou art mindful of him? And the son of man that thou visitest him? For thou hast made him a little lower than the angels and hast crowned him with glory and honor." (Ps. 8:4-5).

Man was crowned with the glory and honor of God. The word crowned means "completely encircled or clothed." Man was clothed in glory. The word "glory" (in Hebrew) is kabowd, which is "the weighty presence of God." Man carried a weighty measure of God's presence and authority. This glory was necessary for him to execute dominion in the earth. When God gives you an assignment, you need His authority and presence to execute it. He was also clothed with honor. The Word honor in the Hebrew means, "magnificence and excellence." Adam was completely clothed with God's weight of authority, radiating with magnificence and brilliance. Yet, when they sinned, the glory and honor lifted off them. This is why the scriptures state that all have sinned and come short of God's glory. (Romans 3:23).

They are lacking God's glory. We are destitute of God's glory. In order to cover their deficiency they sewed fig leaves to themselves in order to cover their nakedness. What were they naked of? God's glory and honor. They tried to cover and conceal their inadequacy. Rather than being clothed with the glory and honor of God they were covered in shame, disgrace, and dishonor. Shame entered into the soul because of losing the glory and honor of God. Their soul was now exposed and experienced disgrace and dishonor, which caused them to run and hide from the presence of God. Shame is like an emotional virus that attacks our soul. Shame can keep a person from ever coming into their full potential. When a person is covered in shame, their potential is blanketed and restrained. Their self-esteem is low. They lose confidence in themselves. With shame comes condemnation.

"There is therefore now no condemnation to them which are in Christ Jesus, who walk not after the flesh, but after the Spirit." (Rom. 8: 1)

Shame is a virus of the soul. When your body has a virus it is infected and becomes sick. When your soul takes a hit, either from any or all of these agents of devastation, you get infected with an emotional virus called shame. Shame can have such a negative effect upon a person's soul that it causes their soul to become sick.

As I have stated earlier, your soul is the seat of your emotions, will, and mind. It is in your soul that your personality resides. It is the place where your preferences lie. When your soul is sick, your decisions are affected. You make decisions from a wounded soul. You make decisions based on the memory of the pain of your past. When your soul is sick, your emotions are affected. You may be experiencing bitterness, anger, regret, or resentment. All of these are symptoms of a sick soul. When you are experiencing these symptoms, it is an indication that your soul has been wounded and damaged. It is important to note that for you to have years restored to you, that you have your soul restored as well.

It is only through the sacrifice of the Lord Jesus Christ that a person can be healed of shame. When Christ was crucified on Calvary, one of the things that the soldiers did was strip Him of His clothing and cast lots for them. This left Christ on the cross, naked and ashamed, one of the most humiliating acts a person had to go through during crucifixion. He rolled away the reproach and bore our shame.

God says for His children to rejoice in advance because although you may be in shame now, you may be in poverty now, you may have experienced devastation and loss now, but My people will never be put to shame again. When God gets through restoring His people, you will never be dishonored again, you will never be disgraced again, and you will never be in lack again. His people will never be ashamed!

Restoring your soul is one of major steps to you redeeming time. David prayed for God to restore his soul. (Ps. 23:3) Part of the process of recovering from missed opportunities is to have your mind, will, and emotions restored. I used to think that time heals all wounds. This is not true. It only prolongs the healing that needs to take place.

I have shown you several ways in which you can begin to move toward a whole and healthy soul, but ultimately God is the one who is going to restore your soul. God is the healer. Time does not heal all wounds, only God can. I am not saying that it is going to be easy and it might not happen overnight, but you can recover your losses and move into your tomorrows with a whole soul. Once you have successfully begun the healing process, you must protect your heart. The strategy of satan is to wound your soul. He cannot touch your spirit. Your spirit has already been made new. It is born again. However, your heart and your soul must be guarded and protected. It must be protected so that no root of bitterness, resentment, or anger takes root in your soul and disqualifies you from future opportunities. Listen, God can present opportunities to you, but if you are not healed from the previous hurts, you will end up disqualifying yourself.

"Keep thy heart with all diligence; for out it are the issues of life." (Prov. 4:23)

King Solomon was emphasizing more than everything else to

guard your heart was. Above everything else, you are to guard your heart. Guard the source of where you make your decisions. Once you have made bad decisions in the past, you will begin to question your capacity to make quality decisions in the future. Your future opportunities are linked with your ability to make quality decisions. Guard your heart from feelings of inadequacy, failure and disappointment. God still has a plan for your life. Your steps are being ordered of the Lord. If you will acknowledge the Lord in all of your ways, He will direct your path (Prov.3:6).

When your soul is restored, you will begin to see God open doors of opportunities and as you move through them will an experience the former rain and the latter rain at the same time. When your soul is restored, you will be in a position like David. *"And David inquired at the* LORD, *saying, Shall I pursue after this troop? Shall I overtake them? And he answered him, Pursue: for thou shalt surely overtake them, and without fail recover all."* (1 Sam. 30:8). You are now in a position of moving from restoration to recovery. Restoration is where your mind, will, and emotions are restored. Recovery is when you get your stuff back. You are now on the road to recovery.

7

Moving into Overflow

WE HAVE COME TO A VERY exciting part of the book that I believe everyone wants to experience in his or her life and that is moving into overflow. The whole premise of this book is to help you understand that when you have lost previous opportunities, you have forfeited the harvest that was connected with the opportunities that God is able to restore to you the years. It is not only about getting the time back, but it is about getting all of the seasons of harvest that were connected to the time.

How is this going to happen? He is going to send two different rains in one season. In other words, He can get one opportunity that has such a profound effect that it brings in exponential return. God will create a season that never existed previously that will move you into overflow. The Scriptures states in Joel 2:24, "*And your floors shall be full of wheat and your vats shall overflow with new wine and oil.*" Up to this point, their floors were empty and their vats were dry. However, when the newly created season was released this was the effect. The outcome and results of having this abundant rain was to produce an overflow harvest.

One of my favorite passages comes out the book of First Kings 18:41. In this passage, the Prophet Elijah says, "*I hear the sound of abundance of rain.*" Elijah could hear something no one else could hear. Elijah could hear what did not exist. The servant could not hear it, neither could he see any evidence of it.

First, abundance has a sound. There is a sound of abundance. Abundance has a frequency. There is the frequency of abundance and is not heard by everybody, and if abundance has a sound, then so does lack. There is a sound and frequency of lack and poverty. People that experience lack are those whose ears have been programmed to the frequency of lack. You have to be recalibrated to sound of abundance. There is a sound of overflow. You have to develop your inner ears to hear that sound. The abundance of rain produces an overflow harvest. This is what Joel is talking about. He is not talking about any type of rain. He is talking about a rain that supersedes all others.

You have to learn to listen for opportunities. Many people miss opportunities because they do not know how to listen for them. Sometimes, before you see an opportunity approaching, you hear one first. You have to learn to listen for opportunities before you see them. Most people miss opportunities because they are too busy looking for them and not listening for them. Develop your inner ear to listen for them. You have to hear the sound of abundance before you see any cloud. The cloud is the manifestation of what you have been hearing in your spirit. If you are waiting to see the cloud before you realize it's going to rain, then it's too late. This is why it is important to have you soul whole; so you can hear clearly in your spirit.

In addition, the louder the sound gets the closer it is to you. This is an issue of timing. Most doors of opportunities are intricately connected to timing. You can be too early for an opportunity as well as too late. Develop a sense of timing through your spiritual hearing. When a person talks about overflow and abundance, usually the first thing that enters into their mind is finances. This shows you where many people's thoughts are. The word overflow in the Hebrew means, "to run after or over, i.e. overflow—overflow, water." Other resources define overflow as the movement of liquid, which has gone over a normal rim or boundary, to be in a state of bountiful excess.

I really like the second part of that definition that says, *to be in a state of bountiful excess.* According to John 10:10, Jesus said that He came that we might have life and have it more abundantly. He came that we might be able to have a continual state of bountiful excess of the God kind of life.

"My heart overflows with a good theme." (Ps. 45:1 NASB)

Overflow must begin in the heart and within your spirit. You cannot have an overflow harvest if you are not prepared internally. God does not want success to destroy you. You have to be bigger than success. Success is not the goal. It is the by-product. The goal is to let men see your good works and glorify God which is in heaven (Matt. 5: 16). Let God build you up on the inside. Let him strengthen you, enlarge you, and anoint you so that everything you do is a result of your overflowing relationship with Him.

"Thou anointest my head with oil, my cup runneth over." (Ps. 23:5). Your life achievements are a result of your overflowing relationship with God. Everything comes out from that relationship. He is the vine, we are the branches, and fruit is the outcome. We cannot produce the fruit. We bear the fruit. Fruit is the result of our overflowing relationship with God.

One of the names of God is El Shaddai, which means, "God Almighty." El Shaddai first appears in Genesis 17:1-2. El means, "The God of power and might." Shaddai comes from the word, "breast." It means provision and abundance. We could translate it "He who is all sufficient." He is the God of more than enough. God is more than enough to meet all your needs in any situation. Look at the impossible need present in this first revelation of the name, "El Shaddai" when Abraham was ninety-nine and Sarah was eighty-nine years old. It was necessary for God to give Abram this revelation of himself in order to fulfill what He spoke to Abraham. Is there something in your life you do not see any God solution? Your God is EL SHADDAI.

Abraham's son, Isaac knew El Shaddai. (Gen. 28:1-3) God revealed himself to Jacob as El Shaddai. (Gen 35:9-11) The word "Almighty" always relates to blessings and multiplication of body, soul and spirit. When Jesus said He came to give us life abundantly, He was speaking as El Shaddai. El Shaddai is used forty-eight times in our Bible, and thirty of those references are in Job. No wonder God revealed himself to Job and doubled his possessions. His accuser friends kept telling him that he must have done something bad, but Job kept calling God "more than enough." You cannot do that in the face of such adversity unless you really mean it.

In Joel 2: 24, the Lord speaks to them and says, *"Your floors shall be full of wheat and your vats shall overflow with wine and oil."* Because of the supernatural rainy season, God was going to cause their floors to be full of wheat and their vats were going to overflow with wine and oil. Remember, this is after the locusts came in and destroyed their crops. Now God says that their threshing floors were going to be full of wheat. Their threshing floors were not going to be empty any longer. They are going to be full. He also states that their vats were going to overflow with new wine and oil.

The threshing floors were places where the grain was threshed and winnowed. The farmer would take the freshly cut wheat and he had a piece of land that was hard to the surface. With a large flat rock in the field, the oxen would pull across the grain and it would crush the shell of the wheat from the kernel of the grain. The farmer would then take a winnowing fork and thrust it into the air the wind would blow away the unnecessary components of the harvest and leave the desired part of the wheat.

On the other hand, the vats were containers of the harvest. Once the grapes and olives were harvested and the liquid was pressed out and drained, it was channeled into vats. So here, we see that both the threshing floors and the vats both were containers that were used to contain the harvest. God said to them that their floors were going to be full of wheat and their vats were going to overflow with wheat, wine and oil.

If you are going to move into overflow, you must have a container for your harvest. Many people miss out what God wants to bring into their lives because they mismanage their harvest. If you are going to move into overflow, it is not going to happen accidentally. It must be the intentional planning and development of systems and strategies in which you are going to manage your harvest. Many people do not know how to capitalize when God sends unusual opportunities because they do not take advantage of them by creating systems that will manage them when they present themselves. You need to have floors and you need to have vats. You need to have a system so that when God gives you opportunities you will have abundance. These containers are necessary to allow your harvest to not be wasted. God does not want your harvest to be wasted. After all, you have been through, and still survived. God is bringing you into a season where you are going to get the former and the latter rain in one month. You had better develop a system so that when it comes you will be able to maximize that system of floors and vats to create a perpetual harvest.

"And ye shall eat the old store, and bring forth the old because of the new." (Lev. 26:10). The living translation states it this way: *You will have such a surplus of crops that you will clear out the old grain to make room for the new harvest!* When you have systems in place to manage your harvest, you will have such residual that you will have to move the harvest from previous seasons into other places so that you can create more space to bring in the new. This will cause you to be creative. You need to develop systems and use your creativity so that you do not miss the chance for the new to come in because you are too preoccupied with the old. This proves to us that there will be such an abundance that the seasons will overlap.

You will still be able to live off the old, but if you do not clear it out, you will miss the new. God wants you to capitalize on seasons of opportunities. In so doing, you will recover years and make up for lost times. If you want overflow and desire to continue to live in a state of bountiful excess, you must take the time to develop systems, which will be a container for a perpetual harvest in your life. You need to develop a system by which one door can initiate other doors or that one door can be a perpetual door. With the perpetual door, you do not just get one harvest but it continues to produce a perpetual harvest of income into your life. God can open one door, but it is up to you to develop the system to bring forth the perpetual harvest.

To remain in a position of continual overflow and residual opportunities, you must develop an attitude of honor and thanksgiving. The Gospel of Luke records an incident were ten men that had leprosy cried out to God for Him to have mercy on them and heal them. Jesus responded by saying, "*Go shew yourselves to the priests.*" (Luke 17:14). And as they went they were cleansed. However, there was one of those men that did something that the other nine did not do. He returned to tell Jesus thank you.

> "*And one of them, when he saw that he was healed, turned back, and with a loud voice glorified God, And fell down on his face at his feet, giving him thanks: and he was a Samaritan. [17] And Jesus answering said, Were there not ten cleansed? but where are the nine? There are not found that returned to give glory to God, save this stranger. And he said unto him, Arise, go thy way: thy faith hath made thee whole.*" (Luke 17:15-17).

All ten of the lepers were healed. However, because one out of the ten returned to give thanks, he received something that the other nine did not receive. The scriptures say that because of him giving thanks he was made whole. He was already healed. But, because of thanksgiving, he received something in addition to his healing. Not only was this man healed, but also his life was made whole. Every area that was affected by this debilitating disorder of the skin that attacked his body, affected his finances, affected his health, affected his relationships, affected his ability to make an income was now made whole. Now, he had received it all back. His finances were made whole, his relationships were restored, and his ability to produce an income was restored. This man received what He asked for, but because he gave thanks, he received more than what he asked for. Every part of his life that the disease affected that was restored.

When God begins to open up new opportunities, do not forget to give God the glory. I know that this may sound simple and foundational. However, many times people get so caught up in the fact that something good has happened that they tell everybody else, but they never return and give God thanks. One way that we can give thanks to God when He gives us new opportunities is to honor Him through our giving of finances. Many people forfeit their harvest because they do not honor God. *"Honour the LORD with thy substance, And with the firstfruits of all thine increase: So shall thy barns be filled with plenty, And thy presses shall burst out with new wine."* (Prov. 3:9-10). Giving of your finances is a way of honoring God. Many people honor God with their lips, but the Bible says that their hearts are far from Him. So, what is the connection between your heart and your finances?

"Where you heart is, there will your treasure be also." (Matt. 6:21). What you value is where you heart will be found. Honoring God is a heart issue that is manifested through giving. You can tell what a person values by how they spend their money. If they value clothing, you will see many expenses from clothing stores. If they value recreation, they will spend a lot of money on recreational activities. If they value God, then they will be financial givers.

God said that when you honor Him with your substance and the first fruits of all your increase, that the results would be your barns filled with plenty and your presses bursting with new wine. Understand that God was primarily talking to an agricultural community. Today, the majority of people do not put their increase in barns or presses. We have checking and savings accounts. This sounds like more ways of developing containers to manage your harvest. To put it in that context, you could say that your checking and savings accounts will be filled with plenty and they will be bursting out.

This truly is a state of bountiful excess. God says to honor Him with the first fruits. The first fruits offering was the offering of the produce from the land, namely, from the first and best crops. The first fruits were given in acknowledgement of God's abundant blessings. This offering also indicated that a much larger crop was to follow. God did not have them give the leftovers, but the first fruits. They were giving God thanks by honoring Him with the first and best of the crops.

Finally, Deuteronomy 8: 18 states, *"But thou shalt remember that it is He who giveth thee power to get wealth."* God tells them to not forget where their blessing came from. In verse 17, He states a warning to not say to themselves that by their own power and strength they obtained their wealth. Giving to God keeps you in a position where you do not think that you obtained your wealth on your own. It is a way of acknowledging to God that if it were not for Him, you would not have been able to move into this position. People that do not give, are people that have forgotten who empowered them to receive. People that honor God through their giving are those that acknowledge it God was who empowered them to get this harvest.

If you want to move into a place of perpetual harvest, be a person of thanksgiving by honoring God through giving.

CONCLUSION

I am persuaded that we are moving into the greatest season of restoration in the body of Christ that we have seen in our lives. Whatever has happened to you in the past that has negatively affected your life does not mean that God cannot redeem those missed opportunities. God holds your times and seasons in His hands. He is the *Time Bender*. God can bend time because He holds your times in His hands. God is able to give you in a moment what you lost in years. Developing a healthy soul are keys to unlocking and restoring time so that when God bends time you will be qualified for your harvest.

Open your spiritual ears and align yourself to listen for the sound of the abundance of rain. You may not see any evidence of rain but there is a sound in your spirit that God is about to bring a harvest that is unexpected. The louder it gets, the closer it is. A season is custom tailored for you. As you prepare for these seasons of restoration, get your soul whole, prepare your containers for your harvest, and continue to be a person who lives a lifestyle of thanksgiving. What God is about to do for your life, you will eat and be satisfied and you will praise the name of the Lord your God because He is who has given you the power to get wealth, create opportunities and recover lost seasons? The *Time Bender* is already preparing and creating a harvest for you that is being released from the eternal into time, it's coming suddenly. Can you hear it?

Made in the USA
San Bernardino, CA
05 August 2014